Phoenix RISING

By Keith W. Sikora

*To Michael
Enjoy the poetry!*

*Keith Sikora
aka Wolfcloud Poet
3/2026*

Copyright Notice

© 2015 by Keith W. Sikora

River Oaks Press

All Rights Reserved

      This is a collective work of poetry. All aspects of the work are a product of the author's imagination and any resemblance to persons living or dead is purely coincidental. This book is licensed and may not be resold or given away. The reproduction, resale, or distribution of this book in whole or part, by electronic or any other means, without the written permission of the author or publisher, is unlawful piracy and is punishable by law. Support of the author's rights is deeply appreciated.

ISBN-13: 978-1519707239

ISBN-10: 1519707231

Website: https://wolfcloudpoet.wordpress.com

Dedication

For Lee Ann

My wife, my sidekick, my muse, my love. Thank you for support, The Lessons, Feedback, Creative Magic, Mystic Technical-ness, and your unwavering belief in me.

Table of Contents

Copyright Notice	2
Dedication	3
Table of Contents	4
Forward: In the Words of a Poet	8
I Want to Fly	9
Home	10
Red Tail Hawk	11
Lifelong Road	12
Mississippi Mojo	13
Unopened Song	15
As Evening Falls	16
When The Sun Rises	17
Pink Floyd	18
Roadside Universe	19
Siren of Wind	20
Solitary Universe	21
My Muse is on Strike	22
Abandoned House	23
What Remains	24
Front Porch Moment	25
Swallowtail Butterfly	26
Nightsong	28
Tide Pool	29
Between Two	30

Heavy Metal Soul	31
A Breath of Faith	33
Love	34
As if I Were the Wind	36
Stars and Stripes	38
Promise of the Sun	39
Courage	40
Mt. 56	41
Forever and Magic	43
The Wee Hours	44
Music is a Part of me	45
Borderline	47
A Span of Space	48
Phoenix Rising	49
Airborne Assault	50
Radiance of Love	51
Making Music	52
Finding My Way	53
Talk	54
Radio Magic	55
Snowflakes II	57
Magic of my Muse	58
Disembodied	60
Monster	61
Liquid Sparks	62
Within	63
The Lesson of Hindsight	65

Miss Maudie's Voice	66
Out Like a Lion	67
God Listens	68
Evening Commute	69
Elemental Force	71
Settled Down	72
Midnight Bus Ride	74
Flying High Again	75
Jungle Rhythm	76
Smoking Thunder	77
Seagull Pt. II	78
Fire!	79
Singular Conversation	80
Later on Sunday Afternoon	81
Goodbye Hugs	82
Barbie World	83
Spotlight	84
The Road Home	85
Last Leg	86
Mississippi Blue	87
All on a Saturday Night	88
Children of the Moon	89
Bone Weary	90
Blessing	91
Girly Twinkle	92
Wildfire	93
College Education	94

One of My Favorite People	95
Road of a Lifetime	96
Altered Destiny	97
Spanning Oceans	98
Trying to Catch the Sun	99
Raven Spaces	100
Learn to Fly	101
Romancing the Night	103
Up from the Wreckage	104
A Psalm of Thanksgiving	105
Acknowledgements	109
Author's Notes and Thanks	111
About the Author	112
Coming Soon	114

Forward: In the Words of a Poet

Why do I write poetry?

Good question. In the words of this poet, I write poetry because I need to, I want to and I like to.

Poetry is a way for me to express my innermost thoughts and feelings that I might want kept private along with being a God given gift I want to share. Writing poetry is my way of expressing to others how I see the world around me and the magic that it contains. Poetry allows me to express that wonder that's both everywhere and within me.

Writing poetry is one way that I increase my knowledge. It is also a constant challenge for me to improve my vocabulary as well as my writing skills. It helps with my personal growth, too. Reading the poetry of others, famous or not, enables me to see through different eyes and to see with a different perspective.

Through poetry, I am a painter. Life and love are my canvas, words my colors, imagery my brushstrokes with the poem my finished piece. Poetry allows me to fly, to dream, to hope, to smile and to cry.

Why do I write poetry?

I write poetry because it's who I am.

Keith Sikora

7/2/2015

I Want to Fly

I want to fly
Find my own wings
Taste all the colors
That sunshine brings.

I want to rise
Like a bird of prey
My feathers like whispers
Upon a windswept stage.

I want to grow
Be a redwood tree
Reaching out for the Light
Plant roots into my dreams.

I want to be lightning
Feel the kiss of that spark
Electrify the night
Keep that magic in my heart.

I want to dance
Like Gene Kelly in the rain
Get lost in that moment
Where there isn't any pain.

I want my soul to shine
Sing bright like sparrow song
Find myself that other heart
Where my love can belong.

I want to be sunrise
Each day a discovery
Sharing with turquoise sky
All that being me means.

Home

2,100 miles
Of sleepless train tracking journey
Passing time
With passenger window views
Through coastline, valley and mountains
Across desert, mesa, Rockies, small towns, cornfields,
Pinewoods, rivers, big cities, day and night
Just to come back to you.

Outside on the front porch
Wrapped up in the gloaming silence
Of a late August dawn
In Glen, Mississippi
Crows caw each other
Somewhere off in the pines
As I stand here
Warm waking coffee in hand
Watching sunrise
While everyone else sleeps
Smiling
My spirit sings
With this tranquil satisfaction
My mind cozy in the confident comfort
Of knowing
My heart is home.

Red Tail Hawk

Red tail hawk
Soaring
The ethereal expanse
Of the wind
Give me
The mojo
Of your ancient dream.

Lifelong Road

(For Lee Ann)

This wonderment of union
Coupling of hearts
Coalescing of spirits
Sparkling with together magic
Into morning sunrise
From across the distance
Of starlight
And crescent moon.

Two
Are now
One
On common ground
In singular purpose
Embraced with shared dream
Heading out on lifelong road
Of love.

Mississippi Mojo

There's an elder energy
Coursing covert within this place.
An ethereal stream
Weaving threads of wild lightning gleam
Across the wooded face
-- Into the denim durability--
Of this land's quiet grace.

It's in the thunderous scream
Of this climate's chameleon mentality.
--Brings that heavy metal rain
Drumming hard until daybreak.
It's in the sauna squeeze
Of summertime humidity.
--Brings that harvest rainbow
Dogwoods & oaks turned to winter's hold.

There's a celestial connectivity
Dancing tribal within this spiritual space.
Deep frying a cascade of creativity
Into the artistic cavalcade
--Braced with the needlework of family--
Found in the handcrafted feel of this faith.

PHOENIX RISING

It's in the belief Jesus always Is
Molded into works the potter's wheel spins
--Brings that watercolor countryside
Back to the eyes of childhood times.
It's in the kindness of Southern charm
And the loved ones kept kindred in our heart
--Brings that sass to this rebel grin
Bonds that nature to this way we live.

There's a wavelength of magic show
Broadcast by birdsong each new morning.
A Mississippi mojo
Buzzing along with the airflow
Cool as dragonfly dazzle on the wing
--That echoes within the soul--
Earthy as the blues we sing.

Unopened Song

Lonely piano
Stashed in the corner
Like a gift left unopened
Give me
The ethereal magic
Of your song.

As Evening Falls

Sunlight glistens
In the July humidity
Dropping golden shadows
On the courthouse lawn
As evening falls
Civil duties give way
To the homebound embrace
Of darkness coming on.

When The Sun Rises

(For Lee Ann)

When the sun rises
That shadow presence
Of the past
Will be in the West
And I will be heading east
Pulling away
From the twisted kiss of control
The acid burning brand of surrender
Having shed these suppressive shackles
Of puppeteered guilt
I am flying high
Leaving that septic caress
Of the Dark
Behind.

When the sun rises
This road of wonder
Taken into tomorrow
Is measureless as Mississippi sky
And I will be on the wing
Soaring into that welcoming sun
My heartbeat
Juiced with the promise of hope
My spirit,
Adrenalized
Will be singing a new song
As this free bird goes diving headlong
Into the precious light of life
Wings spread wide.

Pink Floyd

Spaced within
The timing of silence,
Notes
Float across the transparent matter
Of air
Like autumn leaves
Dancing their Ghost Dance
Upon the November wind.

Cradled inside
Electrified measures,
Notes
Play together
Like the gossamer ballet of snowflakes
Against winter's somber horizon.
Within my mind
Harmony resonates
Metered in rhythm
With my heartbeat,
Singing to my soul
Of ethereal joy.

Roadside Universe

Yellow bright
They radiate the magic
Of wonder
Like stars
Gathered into clusters
Of galaxies
Scattered across a roadside universe
Of meadow green
Daffodils signal spring is here.

Siren of Wind

She is a shadow of air,
Always there.
An alluring sensation of presence
Dancing batwing pirouettes
Along the peripheral edge
Of my consciousness.

She is a siren of wind,
A swirling twister witch.
Euphoria promised,
In the tempest of her kiss,
Incites a shiver of magic within
I can't resist.

She is a specter of breeze,
Cuddling me
With ravenous fingers of amorous need.
Creeping into my cubbyhole of sleep,
She whispers of the thunderbolt ecstasy
That will pillow my dreams.

Solitary Universe

The solitude of this room
Is a universe
I live within
And the silence
Is a black hole
That devours
All of the available light
Leaving
Only darkness
To confide in.

My Muse is on Strike

Leaving in anger
The list crumpled on the floor
My muse is on strike.

Abandoned House

Standing by the side of the highway
Left behind by the seasons
Broken down by the weather
Reclaimed by nature
Occupied by ghost stories from yesterday
Abandoned house.

What Remains

The crowd collected
Slowly moving inside
Under a September sky
Sullen and leaden and bayonetted
With morning's first rays of sunshine.

Silently she mused,
The amount of love here left her surprised
Though she knew the magic of his light.
She knew he'd be happy, too,
Knowing he'd shared it with all these lives.

As the last of the guests
Said goodbye and moved on
She promised to keep calm and carry on
Despite the emptiness
Knowing she would join him in another dawn.

Front Porch Moment

Outside early
In the misty chill
Of these Mississippi woods.
Front porch cup of coffee
Watching
This October sun
Climb slowly over the horizon
Moving into the delicate blue sky.
The bright
Chasing after
The receding night.
My view of the trees
Across the road
Now modified
Into a myriad of shapes
Shaded
In dark and light.
The autumn colors now altered
Left brush-stroked
In muted hues
Of earthen brown, wildfire red,
Evergreen
And sunshine yellow.

The image
Framed by the porch railing and roofline
With the white wooded poles at the sides.

Kodak moment for the soul.

Swallowtail Butterfly

(For Me)

Fluttering,
Wings of shiny yellow
Tiger striped in black
Wander
Into the yard
Drifting
Over the pastel clouds of snapdragons
That stand tall and alert
At the rear of the garden
Next to the backyard fence.
Zigging and zagging
Back and forth
Then fluttering
Up and over the fence,
The wings
Vanish into the summer blue.

But to the little blonde haired boy,
Who's stopped digging
To watch,
The random flight of this Swallowtail butterfly
Brings
The sunshine of magic
To him.

Filled with a wonder
That shines
Like solar fire
Flashing
In his storm gray eyes,
Pure joy

Keith W. Sikora
PHOENIX RISING

Races through his veins
To tickle his heart
And light up
His soul.

Nightsong

The bell resonates
The sound marching
Across the approaching tide of evening
While the sable notes of the piano
Dance in the twilight
Sparkling
Like star shine
Against the cold clarity of a winter night
All wrapped within the electric embrace
Of the guitar
As the strings
Cry homeless tears
Into the solitude of the darkness.

Tide Pool

Within the whispering
Of the night
I arise.
Moving like a ripple
Of nocturnal presence,
I wander
Across a star scattered sea
Of dreams.
Carried along by the tidal pull
Of time
As I explore
Coral reef islands and kelp forest coastlines
Of midnight mindscapes
Along the way
Before eventually washing ashore
Upon the rocks
Of half-asleep awareness
Trapped within
A tide pool galaxy
Of dawn creeping through the window.

Between Two

Amidst the epithets
Hurled
Like lightning strikes
Across the no man's land
Of this room
The anger
Hangs over this space
Like wildfire smoke
Blinding and acrid
Filling up the space
Between two.

Heavy Metal Soul

(For KWS)

Out there
Across the cosmos of a life
Made of memories
Shimmering like stars
Sequins cast upon a clear winter night
I've lived.

Sometimes stowed away
Within spaces of obsidian dark.
Bone weary and bleeding
Bearing the scars
Of lessons learned hard.
Seeking sustenance
In the arms
Of shadows at night
While floating
Dead in the water
An existence left adrift
Struggling
To get back into the light.

Sometimes I sailed the smile
Of summer skies
As a young falcon on the rise.
My bird of prey eyes
Cast upon tomorrow's horizon
My flight feathers
Filled with the breath of heaven
Directed as the crow flies
By a homemade heart set free
To dream.

Out there

PHOENIX RISING

Across the universe of a life
Made of moments
Flashing like lightning
As they move by
Helter skelter
Like hurricane debris on the shoreline
I've survived.

Sometimes facing
Into the howling wail
Of thunder driven wind
Standing like a steel rail
In the path of the approaching gale.
Seeking the presence
Of warmth
Within the polar expanse
Of solitude
Finding only the artic emptiness
Of the cold, instead.

Sometimes I imagined
The words
Of love and life
Through the woodland eyes
Of a shaman poet.
My feelings
Conjured into the verse
Of my being.
Inked those visions
I made mine
Into tattoos of raven
Upon this weathered skin.
Carved them with sunshine
In scrimshaw
Upon this heavy metal soul.

A Breath of Faith

As I walk the unknown path
Of this strange road
Hiking my way
Along the highway to Heaven
I begin to notice
When my days feel out of place
Wearing worry like a chain
Around my soul
That if I take a step back
Take a breath of Faith
And leave it
In the hands of Jesus...

It all goes away.

Love

(For Lee Ann and William)

Love is never conquered

Nor held captive.

Love is a being all its own.

Love will hurt you like the devil

And fly you like a falcon racing across heaven.

Love is a spirit of the wild.

Love doesn't care about the weather, your latest status posting

Or where you're from.

It doesn't obsess over pop culture.

It isn't politically correct.

Love follows only the path it chooses.

Love sees the beauty that all the others missed,

In his goofy smile, in that sparkle flashing in her eyes,

In the sly, knowing wink sent and received by the intended

That goes unnoticed by the rest

At that table of multiple conversations.

Love makes magic of moments.

Love creates weightlessness.

Love sparks the electricity of holding hands.

Love is an elusive creature

That carves its initials into your soul.

Love is not to be measured or defined.

It is to be cherished and shared.

Love is the bond grows of best friends.

As if I Were the Wind

(For Lee Ann)

Embrace me
As if I were the wind.
Holding on
With your fingertips
To the moments of my soul
As they dance their way,
Like moonless stars,
Across the time of your sky.

Embrace me
As if I were the wind.
Take my hand
Let your heart
Run wild
Through the woodlands of my being
As your sunlight magic
Flows like a river into my sea.

Embrace me
As if I were the wind.
Take a chance,
Take this highway
That leads you
Along the journey
Through the galaxies
Of my eyes.

Embrace me
As if I were the wind.
Come along for the ride
Let me be
The wings that carry you

Keith W. Sikora
PHOENIX RISING

Into this sunrise
That waits within the distance
Of my horizon.

Stars and Stripes

(For Those Who Serve and Have Served)

Stars and Stripes Forever
Hanging on a stand
In the corner of the room
Bears silent witness
To all of those
Who have come before
From front line firefight
To quietly civilian behind the scenes.
Honors those who currently do.
And weeps
In solemn remembrance
Of all those
Who gave the ultimate price
For their service.

Stars and Stripes Forever,
As I gaze at your colors
In the corner of the room,
Give me
The enduring dream
Of your freedom.

Promise of the Sun

If I were a hawk
I'd own the promise of the Sun.

Embraced
With the wind
And wing riding the distance,
I'd go chasing after Ra
All the way across the horizon
Until my fair maiden,
The Moon,
Comes rising into the night.

Then, from the secrecy of my roost
High up within the limbs of my tree
I'd gaze upon her wild, mystic beauty
And long for her
With all the love my heart could give
Until once again
The promise of the Sun
Comes for me.

Courage

(For KWS)

Weathered reflection
Of the cloudy day eyes
That gaze back in silence
At this much traveled
Tattoo man,
Share with me
The honesty
Of your shaman magic ...

And give me the courage
To hear
The words you speak
With my heart.

Mt. 56

On the eve of the climb
I stand
In the shadow of Mt. 56.

Looking forward
To making the ascent.
To that first glimpse
Of the other side's horizon.
To standing on the pinnacle.
To watching my step children
And step grand children
Grow...
Into their own being
And the peaks
That they will climb.
To spending the rest of my days
Homesteading love
With my best friend,
My wife.

On the eve of the climb
I stand
In the shadow of Mt. 56.

Looking back
At this road I've travelled.
The places I've been.
The things I've endured; the lessons I've learned.
The miles left behind.
How far I've come.
Where I am now.
And I find
That there's this continuous warmth
Glowing within me these days,

A blissfulness
That makes me smile.
A satisfaction
That makes me thankful
For each new day
From the Lord.
That makes me
Look forward
To my road ahead.

Forever and Magic

Summer sky
Makes me think
Of forever
And magic...

There's a forever
Contained within the endless ceiling
Of pale blue
That creates an endless canvas
For the imagination...

And imagination
Is the magic.

The Wee Hours

Within that space
In the dead of night
Where even time
Hesitates
There's a voice
Inside the silence
That whispers to the soul
Of universal truth
Of the ancient energy
In all things.

And cautions against
Losing contact.

Within the stillness
Of the wee hours
Where even the quiet
Holds its breath
There's a comfort
In the shadow of the bright
That talks to the spirit
Of a universal connection
Of how love
Is a universal light

And issues a warning against
Letting the light
Go out.

Music is a Part of me

(For KWS and Rock)

Music is a part of me
Like the sun
Is to the wind...

It's in my DNA.
in fact,
There's this strand of genes
Devoted solely to music
Inside me,
Kind of my own Library of Congress
Of tunes
With a selfie version
Of the Rock and Roll Hall of Fame
Built in.

Music is a part of me.
It's the soundtrack
To my everyday...

From sunrise 'til moonlight
Rock is at my side
Firing across the neuron roadways
Of my mind
To resonate
Mystical melodies
Down to the core of my being
To pound
It's heavy metal rhythm
Through the rivers
Of my bloodstream
To raise high
It's anthem of power chords
And classic harmonies

Carried as my flag
Within my heart.

Music is a part of me.
It brings me a casserole
Of happy
When my soul is hungry...

Its vision is in the words
Of my poetry.
Its adrenaline fires me up
Elevates my heart rate
Gets my feet to tapping
Sets my spirit to rockin'.
It turns me
Into an air musician...
Guitar and drums
With equal precision.
It's tattooed upon my skin.
It's emotion
Speaks of this love
That I feel
For you.

Music is a part of me.
It's wild gypsy magic
Gets me through...

Borderline

Drifting along
In the twilight zone spaces
Of the thunder laced distance
I gaze at a slate painted sky
Day dreaming
Here on the borderline
Of seasonal change
As the warm southern wind
Gathers up winter's leaves
And tornados them across the yard
As the baby leaves of spring
Dance with glee
Watching winter blow away
Secure in their connection
With the limbs
They wave goodbye in the wind.

A Span of Space

After midnight
When heaven holds kingly court
With its deepest dark sky
To spotlight the sparkle of the stars
That are shining...
There is a span of space
Where time
Stands absolutely still
And the moment
Holds its breath.

Inside
That no man's land
Of silence
Is where
The heart cries
The saddest of tears...

And the steady dripping
Of teardrops
Echoes across the distance of memory.

Falling
Like whispers of autumn leaves
Into the aching black depths
Of the soul.

Phoenix Rising

(For KWS)

When the thunderclouds break
Upon your soul
And the heavy weather
Pounds you
Hard...

It is there
In that solitary moment,
Where the black sky rages,
Lightning fed
And the winds
Come in screaming like Furies,
That the resilience of the spirit
Soars
On wings of sun
And becomes the Phoenix rising.

When hurricane force makes landfall
Upon your shore
And the storm surge
Rushes in
To leave you barren...

It is there
In that breath of space
Between front side and back side
That the courage of the heart
Hangs tough
And becomes the eye of the storm.

Airborne Assault

Transported by a frigid wind
Driven out of the north
Timberland paratroopers
Jump off
Coming down
In an airborne assault.
Attired in the uniform
Of autumn's red, gold,
Yellow and brown,
Woodland warriors
Freefall
Toward their target
Below.
Some go swaying back and forth
Like a baby being rocked before bed.
Some go spinning around
Like an ice skater's pirouette.
Still others come grouped together,
Swirling madly within
A dust devil merry-go-round.
But all of them fall
With a singular purpose,
To cover and conquer
The ground.

Radiance of Love

(A RUSHianku)

lightning fed heartbeats

solar flares speed across skin

radiance of love

Keith W. Sikora
PHOENIX RISING

Making Music

(For Alex, Geddy and Neil)
A RUSHianku

wisdom in lyrics
displayed in musical form
lasting images

Finding My Way

(A RUSHianku)

the journey of life
twists and turns fill the road home
finding my way

Talk

You
Say so much
Within
Such a tiny space.
Every word,
Light as a touch,
Plays a smile
Across my face.

Radio Magic

(For KWS and Rush)
(*Referenced song lyrics written by Neil Peart of Rush)

Early morning gold
Silently creeps
Above the treetop horizon
Of these Mississippi woods
As I
Go rocketing along
I-45
Singing along
To the lyrics
Of one of my favorite songs
By my favorite band, Rush.

"The world is, the world is
Love and life are deep
Maybe as his skies are wide."
The speakers speak
The verses
That hitch a ride
Within the musical stream
Of radio magic
Flowing into my ears.

Early morning gold
Brings a light
That rises and shines
Above the cloud - topped horizon
Behind my eyes
And draws a smile across my face.
Early morning gold
Shares a comforting bright
Which fills my heart
With the radiance of hope.

It sets my spirit flying high
As I
Go rocking along
With the radio magic
Driving down the highway.

"Though his mind is not for rent
Don't put him down as arrogant
His reserve, a quiet defense
Riding out the day's events
The river."
The speakers speak
The verses
That resonate deep within me
Gives me a little clarity
To these visions
Of my life that I dream.
"Though his mind is not for rent
Don't put him down as arrogant
His reserve, a quiet defense..."
The speaker speaks
The verses
To my mind.
Not for rent, indeed.

Snowflakes II

Falling
Earthward
Like little down feathers
From the wings of Angels,
Snowflakes
Come
Wind dancing
Their way down
To briefly
Cover the earth
With a silent quilt
of icebox white.

Falling
Earthward
From a wolf gray sky
Like confetti from Heaven
Snowflakes
Come
In endless geometric designs
Of delicate ice crystals
Courtesy of the Master Creator's magic
To give this gloomy winter day
The wonder
Of a little beautiful bright.

Magic of my Muse

(For Lee Ann)

Sweet voice
That whispers
To me
Inside the horizons
Of my imagination
Like the caress of an afternoon breeze
Held in the arms
Of March,
Speak to me
Of the magic
I have found
Shining
Within the visions
Of your love.

Sweet voice
Of sunshine
That illuminates
My soul
Like the warm embrace
Of April's flowering color,
Share with me,
My Muse,
The mystic power
Contained within your heart.

Sweet voice
That comes
Rocking
At light speed
Along the highways
Inside my mind
Like solar wind

Keith W. Sikora
PHOENIX RISING

Shimmering
Across the wavelength
Of inspiration,
Surround me
With the shine
Of your bright
Like the enchantment
Of stargazing
On a cloudless, chilly winter night.

Sweet voice
Of the siren song
Which holds my heart
In the graceful radiance
Of your smile
Like the paranormal hold
Of full moon glow
Upon lovers below,
Gift me
With the promise
Of your presence
By my side
As I travel
This life long road of mine.

Disembodied

Muffled voices rise
Up from out of the past

Busy
Like yellow jackets
Buzzing,
Echoes of conversation
Coming from disembodied spirits
Resonate
Through the walls

Flowing into my mind
Where my ghosts live.

Monster

If I could any monster,
I would be...

The darkness
That lives within me.

I would have the rage
Of thunder
To fuel my mind.
Lightning would be my reaction.
My defiance,
My shield
Against the invasions I've faced.
The raven spaces
Of midnight
Would be my sanctuary,
And my magic
Would be powered
By the elemental force of tornadoes.

On dragon's wings
I would use the fire
As my strength
Allowing me to keep the Bright
At bay.
Help keep my darkness around me.
Clouds of downpour gray
Would color my eyes
And my claws
Would be made of burning anger.

If I could be any monster,
I would be
The hidden Hyde
To the Jekyll that I see.

Liquid Sparks

On this cold, dismal day
In late February,
Sitting here on my bed
Watching the freezing rainfall
Outside the window
As I write poetry

Staring off into the woods
As if in a trance.
With the enduring drumroll
Of raindrops
Adding some natural background bottom
To the progressive rock
Flowing sweet
From my playlist
Floating Free
Through the speakers in the laptop
Setting my creative meter
Slightly tilted towards darkness.

Yet, listening to the music,
My random thoughts
Stream
Like sunlight glistens
On water.
Liquid sparks of bright
Streaking across these neuron pathways
In my mind.

Keith W. Sikora
PHOENIX RISING

Within

(For KWS and LAS)

Within the nightmares
That haunted me as a child,
Too much time was used
In trying to run away
From those spider web connections
That held me tight
In my dreams.
All of those seasons
Spent chasing after
The ghosts of the days ahead.

Within the thunderstorm
That was my life
As a younger man,
Too much time was wasted
Just cruising down the road.
All those hours
Spent flipping through those photograph moments
Of the scenery flashing by.

Within the fog bank
That surrounded me
As a middle aged dreamer,
Too much time slipped away
While flying in the dark embrace of shadows.
All of those nights
Spent adrift in the doldrums.
All of those long misty days
Spent staring at horizons,
Endlessly gray,
While longing for the love
Of the sun.

PHOENIX RISING

Within the promise of spring
That colors the sky
Of a shaman poet
Pushing sixty,
Too many lessons learned the hard way.
All of these scars
Earned along the way
Are hindsight reminders
Of just how precious is this starlight
Shining within my sight.
The summer comfort of this love
Shared between you and I
Cradles my mornings
With the warmth of your eyes.
Cuddles my midnights
Within the moonshine
Of your smile.

The Lesson of Hindsight

Pewter sky
Filled the color of her eyes.
Gale force winds carry
The echoes
Howling within her laughter.
Longing lost
Still stalks
Through the yesterday hallways
Of her bricked up heart.
Out the window,
The memory horizons
Are overcast
By what could have been.
While the raindrops come
Falling down,
Masquerading
As all of the tears
That she's cried.

Miss Maudie's Voice

Walking to drafting class
On a chill Thursday morning,
My mind
In dreamland mode.
Trying to forget
Winter's last gasp
Still clinging onto the early spring.

Going down the sidewalk
Toward the building of my class,
The repeating birdsong
Of a solitary mockingbird
At the top of a solitary tree
Shines upon the air
Rising
Across the dreary feel
Of this late March morning...

I'm listening with all my heart.

As I pass by the mockingbird's tree,
Miss Maudie's voice
Echoes sweetly within my mind,
"Mockingbirds just make music".
Smiling,
I'm thinking
Miss Maudie's right.

Out Like a Lion

From out of the dominating darkness
Comes a rumbling
So furious
That it shakes the air.
Flashes of shining silver
Hot rod through the coal dark clouds
So quickly
That the clouds shiver.
Flickering brightly
Momentarily,
Before winking out
Into black once more.

From out of the baleful darkness
Comes a rumbling
So wicked
That it makes the clouds cry.
Sweeping by
Tempest winds
Roar in defiance.
Bolts of brilliant electric current
Light up the night
Before blazing
Kamikaze
Into the earth.

The clouds return back to black.

March, going out like a lion.

God Listens

When the mind
Seems adrift
Filled with rainy day haze
When the dreams
The eyes see
Can't seem to find
Their way,
Having been forgotten
In the distance

It is there

Within the echo
Of the desperate silence
That God listens.

Evening Commute

(For KWS and LAS)

Out on the evening road
Rocking along
In my Journey
Woodland trees
Flashing by
With a commuter train blur.
Singing along with "The Spirit of Radio,"
Feeling good
Feeling the magic of the moment
Make the evening mood.
Driving headlong into the colors
Of a slowly setting sun
Feeling the warmth
Of peace
Wash over my soul
Feeling the joy
Of light
Fill my heart
With satisfaction
Cruising across the backwoods boulevard.
Feeling the kiss
Of lightning electricity
Coursing through my veins.
Feeling at ease
With my life.
Feeling glad to be alive.
Sewing my way
Through the twists and turns
Of the countryside.
Car stereo blasting
Some Ozzy
As asphalt gets left behind.

Motoring on my way
To you.

Elemental Force

(For Lee Ann)

As the wind,
My spirit
Comes to you a cat's paw caress.
My desire, this whisper
Sending ripples
Across the water's surface of your skin.

As the wind,
Nursemaids a twister's spin,
This allure of your soul
Howls within me, a vortex of hunger.
My heart, fills with the rain of your tempest.

As the wind,
Carries the eagle's lazy drift,
Riding sky.
This warmth rises inside,
With the zephyr breath of your kiss
Brushed upon my lips.

As the wind,
In serpentine jet stream presence,
My passion flows typhoon intense.
This love, an elemental force
Coalesced within your essence.

Settled Down

(For KWS and LAS)

I'm settled down, now.
Planted my stakes
Upon this patch of land
With you.

As spring arrives
To renew
That enduring circle of life
Within these woods
that circle around our home,
I realize
That I'm in the autumn
Of my own circle.

Taking a breath,
A moment to reflect upon my journey
Along this twisted highway
That has brought me here,
To my life.

Flashing past my thundercloud eyes,
Like a movie trailer,
Moments and memories
Flood my mind
With a meteor shower of images.

Visions of the past,
Of the present
Go streaming by
All mixed up
With those of mine toward tomorrow,
As if in a parade.

Keith W. Sikora
PHOENIX RISING

Lightning bright,
These memories
That I am creating
With you, now,
These are the stories and poems
That we will write down upon the page,
Tag upon our inner walls...
To share with others,
Is the purpose.
To validate our own being,
Brings the cause
To write our own stories.
To record the connections,
Those spider web strands
Of spirit
That we attach to each other.

I'm settled down, now.
Planted my stakes
Upon this patch of land
With you.
I'm at home, now
With you,
Here in my heart.

Midnight Bus Ride

Three quarter moon
Casts a pale shadow
Over the sleeping valley
In defiance
Of the darkness.
Pallid fingers
Stretch across the sky.
Their silver presence
Slithers
Through windows,
Upon blankets,
On walls and floors,
Upon dreaming faces,
Leaving their mark
Of softly glowing moonbeams
Written over the blackness of night.

Flying High Again

(For K44)

Flying high again
Nostalgia
Whispering
Across the evening airwaves
"Eleanor Rigby".
Telling her story.

Flying high again
As if the distance of years past
Had never existed.

Flying high again
The sunlight warmth
Feels good upon my wings.
Flying high again
The joy of memories
Love and a bond
Perpetual as time
Partying
Old School style.

Jungle Rhythm

(For my Cali family)

Jungle rhythm
Running
From the tripod speakers
Early Santana
Rocking magic
Across the windy afternoon.

Sunlight smiles
Cast their presence
Into the traffic of conversation.

Jungle rhythm
Voodoo dancing
In front of the alters
Of burger scented grills.

Sunlight smiles
Made up
In clown face white laced clouds.
Wind driven
They sweep across the Bay Area blue
Like autumn leaves
Caught up in a hurricane.

Smoking Thunder

(For The Fans)

Smoking thunder
Rumbles
Down the track
Roaring defiance
Across the countryside.
Nitro scented air
Filled with images
Of sponsor logos, speed and seconds.

Smoking thunder
Screams
Down the track.
Mechanized lightning
Streaking
Down the lane
To light up the night.

Seagull Pt. II

(For K44)

Seagull, you fly...

Across the sea of time
Upon a breeze of memories
To rock the nation.

Seagull, you fly...

Teary-eyed
Across the sea of pain
To remember
Better days.

Days when the sun shined
Even through the rain.
Days when we shared
The highs,
The lows,
The comfort of each other's company.

Seagull, you fly...

Too rolling stoned
To cross the bridge of sighs.
Still, you fly on
Across the horizon
In your never ending search
For that tropical shore
Where the sun shines warm,
The spirit soars so high,
Where the music never dies.

Fire!

(For Jimi)

Rock
The light
Spirit
The fire
Love
The wings
Fire
The song.

Somewhere high above
Jimi smiles.

Singular Conversation

(For K44)

Sunday afternoon
Relaxed
Listening to new old memories
Chatting around
In a solar system of singular conversations.

As love and nitro
Echo across Sunday afternoon.

Later on Sunday Afternoon

(For K44)

Later on Sunday afternoon
In – between final rounds of drag racing
A solar system of singular conversations
Spinning within their singular orbits
Each a system of its own
Glowing with the shine of peace
Spirits flying along the wavelengths
Of the wind,
Like kite moments
Riding the crest of the airwaves
Across a Sunday afternoon.

Goodbye Hugs

Steely Dan
Drifting Along
The bright birthday blue sky,
Easy as a breeze.
Cool touch of coastal air
Upon sunburn skin
Brings a small smile.

Steely Dan
Drifting along
As the sun strays
Toward the Pacific Ocean,
Heralding the coming of night.
A lingering sense of future anticipation
Mingles
With the wide open embrace
Of a sadness
That clings to the new memories,
Like a shadow in the mist
As goodbye hugs are shared.

Barbie World

(For Leilani)

The little girl
Sitting next to me
On the bus,
Living in her Barbie world.
Rapunzel,
The guest of honor
At the castle ball,
Awaits the servant's assistance
To help her dress up for the dance
As her unicorn pony
Stands ready.

While I
Have become a fashion consultant
To the princess.

Spotlight

Dark night

Bright white

Half full

Spotlight.

The Road Home

(For Lee Ann)

The white lines
Seem to stretch on forever
With a truck stop
At every exit.
The road home
Is lonely and long.
Marked by each stop
In each city
Along the route.
Tracked by each text message,
Each selfie photo,
Each phone call
Along the way
Until the road home ends
When I hold you in my arms again.

Last Leg

(For Lee Ann)

Leaving Dallas
After a three-hour delay
Only added more delight
To the beautiful bright August day
That illuminated
The last leg
Of the long and lonely road home.

With high hopes and Pink Floyd
Playing in my ears
I began to see visions
Of my joyous reunion
With you
Play on the high def screen
In my mind.

As the wheels
Continued rolling down the highway
I ran
Into your welcoming arms.
Holding each other tight
We kissed
Then we looked at each other
With smiles
Big as the August sun.
Eyes sparkling
Spirits rejoicing
Hearts knowing
Together
We are whole
We are home.

Mississippi Blue

(For Lee Ann)

Endless summer sky
Made of Mississippi blue
Reminds me
Of how much love
My heart holds for you.

All on a Saturday Night

(For HOSD)

Dimly lit shadows
Dancing
Fluorescent colors
Radiating ghostly glow
Of purple, green and blue
Across the dark.
Busy bee buzz
Rocking steady
Within the airwaves.
Many faces,
Members of many tribes
Gathered
Under the sky
To pay homage to the Mississippi queen
While the war pigs of many nations
Cried
To their heartbreaker
From Paradise city.
As I returned
Once again
Back in black
To go living after midnight.
All on a Saturday night.

Children of the Moon

A hodgepodge of faces
Flashing spirits
Of fluorescent light
Children of the moon
Howling for their mother.

Bone Weary

Bone weary
Spiritually sore
My travelling days done
Awash in homecoming sun
I think upon days of yore
With a warming smile
Blast from the past
Coming back around at last
To become
Part of the spiritual shine
Held within my present hands
Shining in my grateful heart.
The love
Streaking like lightning
Across the thundercloud skies
Of these shaman poet eyes.
The magic
Dancing around
Like snowflakes
Underneath a starlit night
Inside the universe of my mind.

Blessing

(For Lee Ann)

You
Remain
With me
Long after you've left.
The scent
Of you
Lingers everywhere.
The echoes
Of your sunshine laughter
Keep playing
Over and over
In my ears
Like some ancient magic chant.
You
Are like a soft spring breeze
Whispering
Your song of enchantment
Throughout the canyons
Of my mind.
You
Are the one
That I've traveled
Upon this serpentine path
For so long
To find.
You
Are many things,
Wife, mother, Dodo, partner, sidekick,
Muse, teacher, and best friend.
You
Are my blessing.

Girly Twinkle

(For Lee Ann)

That girly twinkle

Within those beautiful blues

Of yours

Is like looking into

A clear summer night.

Starlight sparkling above,

But it's the moonlight,

Shining silver

Upon the tidal crests

As the sea

Comes steadily washing ashore

That catches my eye.

Wildfire

(For Nancy)

She bubbles and boils
As she flows
Through the gravitational pull
Of the moments she creates.
Simmering
Like magma
Burning just below the surface.
She goes rocking on
Through the twists and turns
Of her todays,
Carving her own path
Through the underground
Of the seasons
She has embraced.

She blazes a trail
Like wildfire
As she dances
Upon the eastern wind.
Fire tornado pirouettes
Light up
The night around her.
Her untamed heart
Leaves a memory
Bright
As a firestorm horizon
Across the darkness.

College Education

(For KWS)

Here at the edge
Of the ending of summer
I'm chilling, as usual
Though my mind is a bit scatterbrained
At this moment.
School starts again on Monday.
I'm here
On Thursday evening
Watching the August sun
Slowly lose its grip on the sky.
Waiting for you to end your shift at work.
Thinking of school and being sure
I'm ready for Monday.
Thinking, here I am at fifty-seven about to start
My second semester of college,
The fall semester of my freshman year.
It amazes me
That I'm in college at all,
Much less that I'd be doing this good
With my grades.

That degree is within sight.
The cap and gown walk to receive
My diploma...
At the age of fifty-eight.

One of My Favorite People

(For Jean)

The joy was instant
The moment
You walked through the door.
The love was genuine
Flowing happily
Between embraced arms.
The hug was warm and welcome
Shared by
You and I.

Road of a Lifetime

The road of a lifetime
Is winding and rough
Rolling across the seasons
Chasing after the sun
All the while
Caught up within the tidal pull
Of days passing by.

Tomorrow is a vision
Elusive within the haze
Hunted down yet never found
Because it's always today.

The mountains that we climb
Are rugged and steep
Still uphill, through the mist we reach
For the peak and those stars we seek
As the horizon flies
Away, like some faded memory,
Into the embrace of the night.

Time is an ocean
Fed by rivers of life
Life is a radiance
Filled with celestial light.

Altered Destiny

Blending into the morning traffic

Of worker bees

Swarming down the sidewalks

Rushing along

Like a living river

Through the skyscraper canyons,

The ninja presence

Like a breeze in passing

Flows along calmly

With the current of the crowd,

A shadow

Within a shadow

On a course

To forever change their destiny.

Spanning Oceans

(For Doris)

From across the span of the ocean
That once held Atlantis,
Your voice speaks to me
With written wavelengths
Of mystic vision.
Framed inside the measurements
Of time's signature
Your husky mockingbird melody
Brings a siren's call
Filled with the colors
Of guitar, bass, flute and violin
That shine
Like a star littered night
Within the woodlands
Of my mind.

From the land of Purple Haze and the Mississippi Queen
To the United island kingdom of Merlin and Rihannon
I reply
With the lightning bright fantasy
Of free verse images
Written with this poet's eyes.

Trying to Catch the Sun

Flashing

Lightning

Bolts across the thunderstorm skyline

Of my eyes

Briefly

Illuminating

Moments and memories

Left behind in the distance

Of hindsight

From a life

Spent trying to catch the sun.

Raven Spaces

Within the solitude

Of my soul

Like a lost spirit

Roaming

The raven spaces

In between

The night's silence

And the visions

Of dreams

Whispers

Of a lone wolf

Still linger

Yearning for the embrace of the moon.

Keith W. Sikora
PHOENIX RISING

Learn to Fly

(For KWS)

Painted
Within the pencil black brush strokes
Of stories told
Upon a canvas
Of yesterdays
Spent chasing after the wind
While trying to learn
To fly.
The lessons of youth
Were razor sharp
Cutting deep
Learned the hard way.

Animated
By the electricity
Of freedom
Looking for my own
As a young hawk.
Trying to ride the lightning
While seeking shelter
Within the storm
Ended
Dancing in the darkness
Swept away
By the vortex.
Left grounded
Burnt out and fried.

Rolling
Across the years of winter time
Inside my mind

Shimmering waves
Of solar fire
Wash over the night sky
Of these dark matter dreams
With dazzling color display
From horizon to horizon.
Images of insight
Hiding
Within the moon shadows.

Sketched
Upon the parchment of seasons passing
The memories
Of a night bird on the wing
That lost his direction
Somewhere on his migratory path
Wandering through the hazy clouds
Until he nosedived and crashed.

Romancing the Night

Across the span of seasons spent
As a dreamer
Romancing the night
Moments shared
In the summer warm embrace
Of her sparkling darkness.
Held spellbound
By the diamond bright
Of her constellation eyes.
Content within the chorus of night sounds
And in each other's presence
Until autumn arrived
Cloaked in the cold solstice shadow
Of winter
And the night
Sent me away
Riding bareback on a comet tail
On a journey
Looking for my spirit's kindred light.

Up from the Wreckage

Rising

Back up from the wreckage,

An enlightened Phoenix,

To ride the thermal currents

Of forever blue sky.

Leaving a vapor trail

Of the past

Behind.

Embraced within the warmth of love

Bathed in the shine

Of her smile.

Soaring high

Heading home

Into tomorrow's sunrise

Flight feathers opened wide.

A Psalm of Thanksgiving

(For God)

Hear me!
Oh Lord, my God,
Hear my prayer of thanksgiving,
For You are the God of my salvation!
Mighty Redeemer,
I give you praise
For You have blessed me
Through all of my days.

Listen to the words of my heart, Heavenly Father,
For this heart
Has known the cold solitude of sadness.
My soul has known the silent loneliness
Of one
Who has been tribe less for so long.
Like a cedar tree
Existing within a colorless desert, barren of rain.

I now know that I was not alone.
For You, my creator,
Have been with me
Throughout this earthly journey.
Even as I stumbled my way
Along this treacherous trail.
Through my wilderness walk across the valley
Of the shadow of death,
You were there by my side,
Just waiting for me to open the door
To my heart.

Oh, King of Kings, You are my champion!

Keith W. Sikora
PHOENIX RISING

Your righteous shield of grace and mercy protects my soul.
You kept my heart stout against the burning arrows
Of pain
Caused by those who chose to beat me repeatedly
With oppressive anger.
You sheltered me against those
Who threw the scalding stones
Of poisonous words at me
With each new sunrise.

Because of Your strength within me,
My steadfast guardian,
I raised myself back up every time I was struck down.
Through You,
I have a spirit that cannot be broken.

My God of all that is good, You are my shepherd.
You have sent me an angel down from Heaven
To watch over me.
You brought me back from my youthful foolishness.
You kept me from falling away into the night.
You were the light
That kept me from being blinded by the black.
You prevented me from becoming lost
Every time I danced along the edge of darkness.

You brought me home.
You made me your child.
You give me the lessons of Your Word
To hold close to my heart and mind.
You forgive me my trespasses.
You showed me that I am worthy.
You have blessed me with the love of my precious wife
Along with this loving family of faith.
A blessing far beyond all the worth of mortal material
riches.
You are the wonder of all wonders.

Keith W. Sikora
PHOENIX RISING

My life is brighter because You dwell within it.

Oh Lord, my King of Light,
Maker of all the stars sparkling up in the night sky,
You are my universe!
Your radiance shines within these storm gray eyes.
You are the cause of my creativity.
You are the spark of my inspiration that allows me to express
What my spirit vision sees within the miracle
Of all of Your creation around me.

I am so grateful for the blessing of this poetic magic
You have gifted me with.
So I have written this Psalm for You, my Lord.
I humbly offer it in Your honor.

My King of Heaven, I am Your living sacrifice.
You have my heart and soul, freely given to You
By this humble servant.
Holy Father of mine,
The swift sword of Your Holy Spirit
Along with the cross of Jesus
Are tattooed on the sleeve of my flesh,
Engraved upon my heart as a tribute
To Your everlasting glory.
My love for you is given complete, as is my faith.
For You have filled me with a perpetual joy, so powerful,
That it brings tears of gratitude to my eyes.
For Your love for me is unlimited, this I know.

My precious God,
I pray when the day comes
When my flesh no longer matters,
That I find my spirit surrounded with Your eternal light,
In the company of my loved ones.
All of us gathered together

In Your glorious kingdom of Heaven,
Forever.

Acknowledgements

1. What Remains – "Writing in the Crossroads" Anthology, Crossroads Poetry Project, April, 2013, Saturday Poems and Their Stories Blog – www.wolfcloudpoet.wordpress.com , Oct. 2015.

2. Front Porch Moment – "Writing in the Crossroads" anthology, Crossroads Poetry Project, April 2013

3. Tide Pool – "Illuminate Our World with Poetry" anthology, Crossroads Poetry Project, April, 2014

4. Nightsong – "Illuminate Our World with Poetry" Anthology, Crossroads Poetry Project, April 2014

5. Between Two – "Illuminate Our World with Poetry" Anthology, Crossroads Poetry Project, April 2014

6. Airborne Assault – "The Magical World of Poetry" Anthology, Crossroads Poetry Project, April, 2015

7. Phoenix Rising -- "The Magical World of Poetry" Anthology, Crossroads Poetry Project, April, 2015; and Saturday Poems and Their Stories Blog – www.wolfcloudpoet.wordpress.com , Nov. 2015.

8. Monster -- Saturday Poems and Their Stories Blog – www.wolfcloudpoet.wordpress.com , Oct. 2015.

9. The Lessons of Hindsight - Saturday Poems and Their Stories Blog – www.wolfcloudpoet.wordpress.com , Oct. 2015.

10. The Road Home -- Saturday Poems and Their Stories Blog – www.wolfcloudpoet.wordpress.com , Oct. 2015.

11. Spanning Oceans -- Saturday Poems and Their Stories Blog – www.wolfcloudpoet.wordpress.com , Oct. 2015.

12. Red Tail Hawk -- Saturday Poems and Their Stories Blog – www.wolfcloudpoet.wordpress.com , Dec. 2015.

13. Unopened Song -- Saturday Poems and Their Stories Blog – www.wolfcloudpoet.wordpress.com , Dec. 2015.

14. Courage -- Saturday Poems and Their Stories Blog – www.wolfcloudpoet.wordpress.com , Dec. 2015.

Author's Notes and Thanks

- K44 – The Sonoma Raceway Campsite Space Number of the legendary family group of my friends out in the San Francisco Bay area.
  The group members are: Ron & Laura; Kenny; Nancy & Miles; Troy; Al & Susie; Mikey; Carol; Mario; and Tom the Cat.

- www.wolfcloudpoet.wordpress.com is my weekly blog – "Saturday Poems and Their Stories. Stop by and visit if you can!

Special Thanks
- Robb & Michelle, Sean, Tracy and Darrin, - my family out West – thank you for all your support, encouragement, and your steadfast belief in me... I DID IT YA'll!!!

- The Crossroads Poetry Project – Thank ya'll for all you do to help kids read, write, and love poetry in all the county schools. Board members are: Autry, Cody, June, Lee Ann, myself, (Sorry if I missed anyone) and a very special thanks to the late Donna Stockton (our founder)

About the Author

Keith Sikora is a shaman poet and a Pisces who sees magic in everything around him. Keith began writing poetry in 1976, continuing to compile binders of poems since. He had his first paid published poem,"Faerie," in 1998.

   He won an Honorable Mention award for his poem, "Branches and Roots," in the 1999 Writer's Digest poetry competition and in the same year won the $500 Editor's Favorite Award for his poem,"Lord Tiger Of The Snow," in the Quill Books anthology, "A Time To Be Free." His poetry has been published in several other anthologies as well. He placed third and Honorable Mention in the Crossroads Poetry Project's 2013 poetry contest with his poems, "What Remains," and "Front Porch Moment." In 2014, Keith took first, second and an Honorable mention with his poems, "Tidepool," "Nightsong," and "Between Two," in the Crossroads Poetry Project's contest. In 2015, he took third place and Honorable Mention with his poems "Phoenix Rising," and "Airborne Assault."

   Keith's first book of poetry,"Voices Of Light," was published in 2000 by Tiger Moon Press and the first edition is available at -
www.tigermoonpress/search/Voices of Light/ The first edition of his second poetry book, "Celestial Bodies," was published by Sam's Dot Publishing in 2011. Now available at Alban Lake Publishing.
www.http://store.albanlake.com/page/6/= "Lifelong Road," (coming soon/River Oaks Press) will be Keith's third poetry book.

   His work has been published in magazines, both in print & online, including Aoife's Kiss, Beyond Centauri, Bloodbond, Bubbaku, Champagne Shivers, ETOU, Expressions Newsletter, The Fifth Di..., Frostfire Worlds, Hungur, Illumen, Mobius, Red Owl, Scavenger's

Keith W. Sikora
PHOENIX RISING

Newsletter, Scifaikuest, Shadowland, Sounds Of The Night, Tribal Soul Kitchen, Trysts Of Fate, The Modern Art Cave, and The Moonlit Path. Keith is a member of Imagicopter, a website that helps local genre artists, poets and writers promote their work. He is also a member of the Crossroads Poetry Project, a non-profit group that promotes the reading and writing of poetry for children in local schools. He also teaches poetry workshops for the Crossroads Poetry Project.

When not hunkered down in his creative sanctuary listening to Heavy Metal and Progressive rock and writing poetry, Keith enjoys teaching Free Verse and Speculative poetry workshops, collecting Hot Wheels cars, reading, taking photographs of weather and nature wherever he wanders, talking to wild critters, and hanging out with his five mischievous canines, Jojo, Rosalie, Weiner, Rocky, and Dio. Keith lives in his own little universe happily married to his Muse, Lee Ann.

Keith W. Sikora
PHOENIX RISING

Coming Soon

CELESTIAL BODIES

(Second Edition)

By Keith W. Sikora

Made in the USA
Charleston, SC
19 February 2016